BEGINNER'S GUIDE TO HANDBUILDING

LEARN HOW TO CREATE SLAB POTS, MUGS, PINCH POTS, COILED POTS AND OTHER AMAZING CERAMIC ART WORK LIKE A PRO

ANNA SPILLMAN

Made with ♥ on the Notion Press Platform
www.notionpress.com

This book is dedicated to God and to my wonderful family for their unwaving support

Contents

CHAPTER ONE

Handbuilding Pottery Guide

Clay is a material rich in history and artistic potential, and handbuilding pottery is the medium's first use. The Ceramics Department at The Crucible is a one-of-a-kind location for learning the various handbuilding pottery skills of pinching, coiling, and slab rolling. Once you've mastered a few fundamental methods, you may create useful dinnerware, containers, sculpture, installations, and mixed media pieces—the possibilities with ceramics are limitless.

How is handbuilding defined?

Handbuilding is a ceramics method that utilizes clay and your hands to make shapes without the need of a throwing wheel. Prior to the invention of the wheel, ceramicists could only make utilitarian and aesthetic ceramic shapes by handbuilding. The earliest known ceramic item was made by hand and dates all the way back to 28,000 BCE. To get started, all you need is clay, your hands, and a few basic tools.

Methods and techniques for handbuilding

While handbuilding is as basic as making an item out of clay with your hands, it involves three distinct techniques and forming procedures. Once you've mastered pinching, coiling, and slab construction, you can create almost anything out of clay.

Pinching Pots

Pinch pots are an excellent initial handbuilding technique to master while working with clay for the first time. Simply take a single ball of clay and form it into a little pot by pushing your thumb into the middle of the ball. With one hand, hold and spin the ball while pressing the walls out with your thumb. Pinch pots are an easy way to begin working with clay and familiarize yourself with the material.

Enter Caption

Coiled Pots

Coiled pots are formed by rolling out long, separate coils of clay and connecting them to form a bigger piece. Coiled pots come in a variety of shapes and sizes. Additionally, you may combine the pinch pot and coil pot techniques by pinching a shallow dish to serve as the basis for your coiled pots. Continue to add coils to your item until you are pleased with the shape and size.

Slab pots

After they have been processed by a slab roller, a slab pot is made by connecting flat slabs of clay together. Slab rollers, which are essentially industrial-sized rolling pins, are an excellent instrument for producing clay slabs quickly and efficiently.

To begin, put your clay on the slab roller's fabric and spin the wheel to move it through. Then, cut the slab to the appropriate size using a sharp tool. You may create paper templates to use as a guide for planning your project and cutting the slab appropriately. Additionally, you may use a slump mold to achieve consistent forms for items like as plates and bowls. Roll out your slab and lay it over or within your shape in this example. Finally, you'll use a procedure called "score and slip" to link the two slabs together. Scratching your clay entails making markings on the two surfaces that will be bonded. Following the scoring, brush slip on either side as if bonding the sides together.

CHAPTER TWO

Materials and tools needed to begin handbuilding process

Handbuilding pottery, you will need just a few ingredients and equipment. There are a few required materials, such as clay and a kiln, as well as other optional tools that may be used to give texture and depth to your sculptures.

Enter Caption

- **Clay**

Use earthenware clay that is sturdy and simple to mold for handbuilding. Keep it wet by storing it in a plastic bag. Premixed, damp clay is the simplest to deal with. If you live in the Bay Area, Clay People in Richmond is an excellent source for professionally manufactured clay. Additionally, you may purchase clay online from a company such as Laguna Clay Company.

- **Cutter for Wire**

Clay is often offered in bulk quantities weighing between five and fifty pounds. When you initially begin your craft, cut tiny bits of clay from your bigger piece with a wire cutter. Keep your clay bag tight while not in use to prevent it from drying out.

- **Pinning tool**

A pin tool is a pointed implement that is used to carve, puncture, and incise patterns into the surface of clay, imparting an unusual texture. Numerous ceramicists also use repurposed dental instruments to provide a particular roughness to the surface of their work.

- **Calculator**

When handbuilding, scoring tools are required to put slabs together. Prior to applying slip, score the clay pieces that will be joined together to ensure that the slip penetrates the clay and joins the two pieces.

- **Rolling slab and canvas sheets**

A slab roller is used to roll out clay slabs to an equal thickness in preparation for slab construction. If you do not have access to a slab roller, a rolling pin and two canvas sheets combined with some muscle would suffice.

Enter Caption

- **Wheel for banding**

You'll set your clay on a banding wheel to simply spin it and make working on your sculpture simpler. This is particularly useful when working with bigger coiled sections or when attempting to create homogeneous textures.

- **Brayer**

A brayer is useful for smoothing out and rolling out the edges of your clay, particularly the lips of bowls and cups. Additionally, by impressing things between the clay and the brayer, you may give roughness to the clay's surface. [Photo: Ceramics I lace texture]

- **Templates**

Create patterns for crafts by cutting templates from heavy stock paper. When handbuilding, templates make it simple to recreate a product.

• **Rib made of rubber**

Rubber ribs are critical instruments for smoothing the clay's surface.

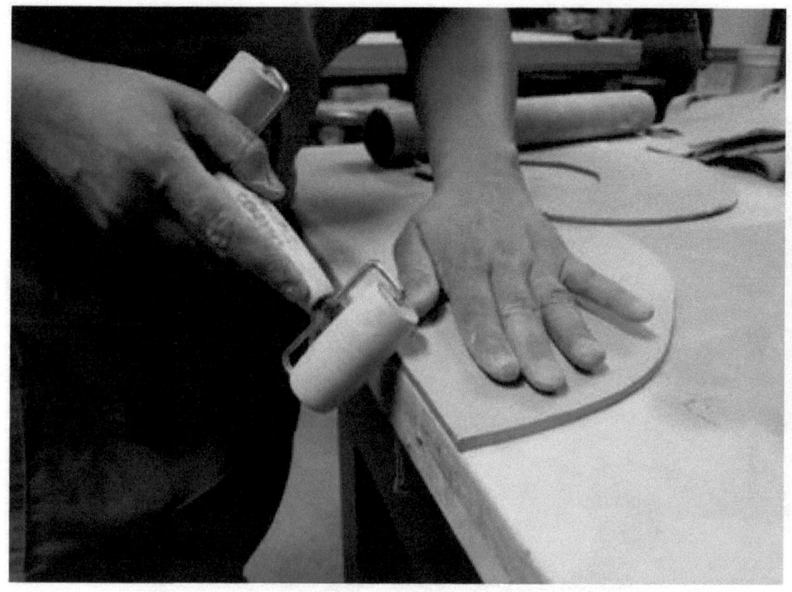

Enter Caption

• **Fettling Knife**

Fettling knives are used to cut slabs of clay quickly. Additionally, these knives may be used to trim, carve, and embellish.

• **Aerosol Spray Bottle**

While working with your clay, keep it wet by spraying it with a spray bottle filled with water.

• **Sponge**

A wet sponge moistens and smooths the clay's surface.

• **Kiln**

To heat ceramic work, a kiln is utilized. A kiln may take around 8 hours to heat up to approximately 2000 degrees Fahrenheit, and another 12 hours to cool down, depending on the job and clay type. If you do not own a kiln, several ceramic studios provide pay-to-fire services in which they will fire your works for you. You'll need to know the cone level of the glaze you're using and ensure that the studio is capable of firing your work at the appropriate temperature.

While The Crucible does not currently provide pay-to-fire services, students are free to utilize our studio's kilns and glazes for their own projects during The Crucible's Ceramics Labs. If you're looking for pay-to-fire services in the Bay Area, check out Potters Studio in Berkeley or Merritt Ceramics in Oakland.

Learning handbuilding

My trainees create sculptural and practical structures in clay using traditional hand-building and surface treatment methods. You may begin with basic programs such as Ceramics I to learn the fundamentals of handbuilding, or enroll in a 3-Hour Taster to sample a new art form without committing to a full semester. Once you've mastered the fundamentals of handbuilding, we offer a selection of advanced handbuilding courses. Pinch and coil a big planter or sculpture in Large Ceramic Forms. Students in our Raku workshops learn a unique fire procedure in which ceramic objects are removed from the kiln while still burning hot and put in an oxygen-depleted environment, imparting vibrant hues to your glazeware.

handbuilding pottery

CHAPTER THREE

Handbuilding Frequently Asked Questions

Which clay is best for handbuilding?

Due of its hardness and fluidity, earthenware clay is the perfect clay for handbuilding pottery. Other clays, such as porcelain, are not advised for starting handbuilding because to their stiffness and difficulty in shaping. Additionally, you may use grogged clay, which includes a high concentration of alumina and silica, which reduces shrinkage and protects your work from breaking during the fire process. Additionally, the grog gives strength when constructing bigger parts.

What is clay handbuilding?

Handbuilding with clay enables the creation of ceramic shapes without the use of a wheel.

How should clay be prepared for handbuilding?

Before you begin building your project with clay, you must knead it, a process referred as as wedging. Kneading clay makes it simpler to deal with and helps maintain an even moisture level. Additionally, it removes any trapped air bubbles that may have occurred during the mixing or recycling of the clay.

What are the three handbuilding techniques?

Pinching, coiling, and slab building are the three ways of handbuilding. Once you've mastered these three techniques, you can create almost any thing out of clay. It's beneficial to begin with pinching and progress to coiling before going on to slab building.

Is it possible to undertake handbuilding without a kiln?

Handbuilding without a kiln is possible or not depending on the kind of clay used. If you're using a self-hardening clay, you may let it to dry overnight rather than firing it. Additionally, there are kid-friendly polymer clays that may be baked in the oven. The disadvantage of various varieties of clay is that your ceramic artwork will have a restricted range of applications. This style of ceramic item cannot be used to eat or drink from.

If you're working with earthenware clay by hand, heat it in a kiln. Ovens are insufficiently hot to fire earthenware pottery, and heating the clay without care might cause it to break. A kiln may take around 8 hours to heat up to approximately 2000 degrees Fahrenheit, and another 12 hours to cool down, depending on the job and clay type.

CHAPTER FOUR

How to Glaze Ceramics and Pottery

Ceramic glazes are an impermeable layer or coating added to bisque-ware ceramics. They are used to embellish and protect the piece. Glazing pottery and ceramics opens us a world of possibilities, from vibrant patterns to mineral reactions.

Glazing ceramics is generally accomplished by mixing glazes, putting them on bisque-ware, allowing them to dry, and lastly placing them into a kiln for glaze fire. The kiln is gradually brought up to the temperature required for the silica in the glaze to melt and then gradually cooled again. This strengthens and solidifies your pottery, making it impenetrable to water and the weather.

Glazing ceramics has the practical function of making them food-safe and waterproof. Once-baked clay bisque-ware is neither waterproof or food-safe until the glaze is applied and then fired again.

How to use a kiln to glaze pottery

Step one

As much as possible, keep your bisque-fired piece clean. Before you begin, use a clean sponge or mildly moist cloth to remove any dust. If you clean your bisque ware with water, ensure that it is absolutely dry before glazing.

Step two

Combine your glazes well. Assemble the heavier sediment, which has probably sunk to the bottom of the mixing jar, to guarantee a smooth consistency. This may be done by hand by aggressively whisking for at least 1-2 minutes. Numerous ceramic studios use a whisk attached to a drill to swiftly and completely mix their glazes.

Step three

Decide how you're going to apply your glaze. You may glaze your bisque-fired ceramics by dipping them in the glaze, pouring it on, or brushing it on.

In ceramics workshops at The Crucible, we utilize underglazes to add color and design before sealing and waterproofing the ceramics with a layer of glaze. Underglazes include a trace of gum, which aids in their control when applied to ceramics. Two to three coats are recommended. Ensure that any glaze on the base of your piece is removed before placing it away to dry.

Step 4

Fire the glaze according to the manufacturer's directions. Glazes are categorised as low-fire or mid-fire, and firing them at the incorrect setting may result in the breakage of your work.

Low-fire glazes are burned at an elevated temperature of 1845 degrees Fahrenheit. Low-fire glazes are ideal for creating very precise, controlled designs. The resultant hues may be vibrant and predictable, and they do not mix very well.

At 2192 degrees Fahrenheit, mid-fire glazes are burned. Colors have a greater range of shades and blend together to produce more romantic visual effects.

The high-fire glazes are burned to a temperature of 2305 degrees Fahrenheit, resulting in a robust, vitreous ceramic. The color palette is often more restricted.

Enter Caption

How to glaze ceramics at home with a do-it-yourself kiln

Glazed ceramics must be burned in a kiln to melt the silica and flow and fuse the glaze to the ceramics. You may construct your own kilns for burning pottery at home in a variety of methods. Always use caution and seek expert assistance if necessary.

Pit Firing

Dig a hole at least one foot deep in your yard and construct a fire inside it using kindling and wood. Temperatures in pits may reach up to 2,000 degrees Fahrenheit. Prepare to spend at least six hours firing your ceramics. You may add patterns and color to the pit by adding various metal oxides, salt, or even by lowering the quantity of oxygen in the pit.

Using Brick Kilns

Similar to pit burning, brick kilns may be employed. You may dig a pit fire hole and line it with bricks, then construct your fire within the bricks. Alternatively, you might construct an elevated brick kiln to fire your pottery. When selecting the material for your brick kiln, it is advised that you utilize fire bricks rather than construction bricks to avoid cracking during the burning process. As you construct your kiln, you may add inside shelves to hold your pottery while it flames. Create an internal fire in the same manner as you would for a pit firing. You may unload the kiln after it has cooled, which typically takes around twelve hours.

Enter Caption

Barrel Kilns

Barrel kilns are a process similar to pit firing in that they use a barrel to contain the fire and ceramics. Begin by drilling many holes in the base of a steel garbage can to allow for ventilation, and then erecting a gravel foundation. Then, put a flammable item on top of the gravel, followed by a layer of pottery, and continue in this fashion. Additionally, you may sprinkle metal oxides and salts on your pottery to alter the color and create surface pattern.

Raku Kilns

To construct a raku kiln, the easiest method is to utilize a small steel garbage can with a sealable cover. Ceramic fiber is used to line the interior of the can and is secured using nickel-chromium wire. Make a tiny hole in the bottom of the can to allow the heat source to pass through. A propane torch with a push-button ignitor attached to a propane tank works effectively and reaches temperatures of up to 3000 degrees Fahrenheit.

Connect a thermocouple to your kiln to determine when it hits 1800 degrees Fahrenheit. Load your pottery into the kiln, switch on the gas, and hold it at 1800 degrees for five minutes. Remove the lid carefully with tongs and carefully transfer your red-hot pottery from the kiln to another small garbage can loaded with flammable debris. To create a reduction environment, cover this little container with a lid and chill your piece in the open air. Bear in mind that raku pottery is not impervious to water or food.

CHAPTER FIVE

Instructions for Making Clay Coil Pots

Coiling clay pots is a straightforward method that involves adding coils or other forms one by one and then welding the layers together to make a solid structure. It is a very adaptable method that is suitable for novices but also capable of producing exceptional workmanship and creativity. Even people who are new to clay should be able to use the coiling process to create huge and fascinating ceramics.

Step 1: Selecting the Appropriate Clay for Coiling

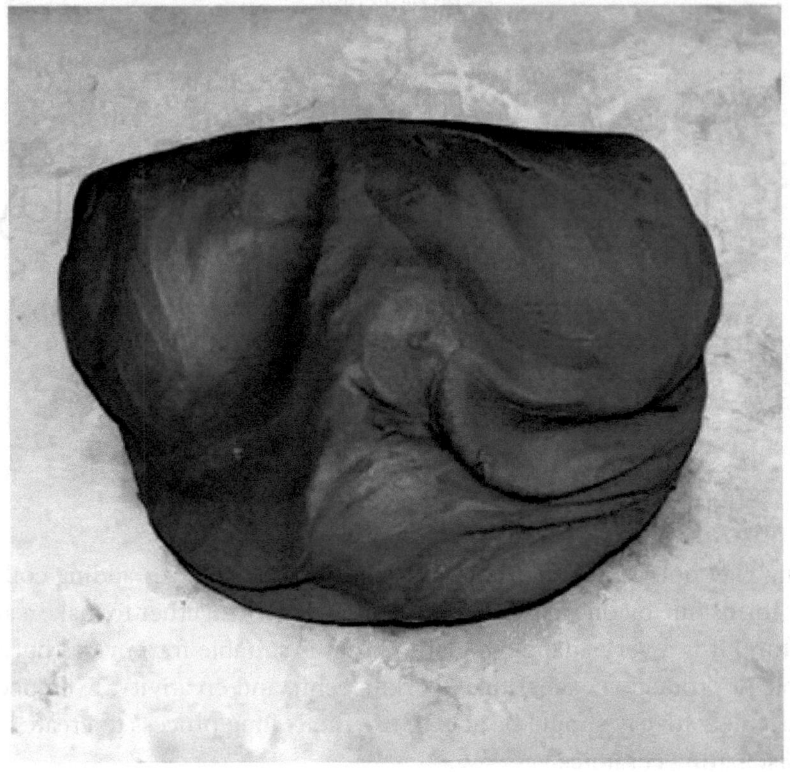

Enter Caption

The clay body used to construct coil pots must be proportionate to the final shape, which means that bigger constructions need greater strength and thicker walls; thus, pick a clay body with an adequate strength and a low coefficient of expansion.

Clay bodies with sand or grog perform the best. Look for a shrinkage rate of less than 8%. Additionally, the clay should be of a soft consistency. Stiff clay does not weld as effectively as soft clay, resulting in weaker joints that are prone to cracking.

Before using the clay, ensure that it is completely wedged. This will homogenize it and eliminate any air pockets that might result in kiln blowouts.

Step 2: Creating the Floor of the Coil

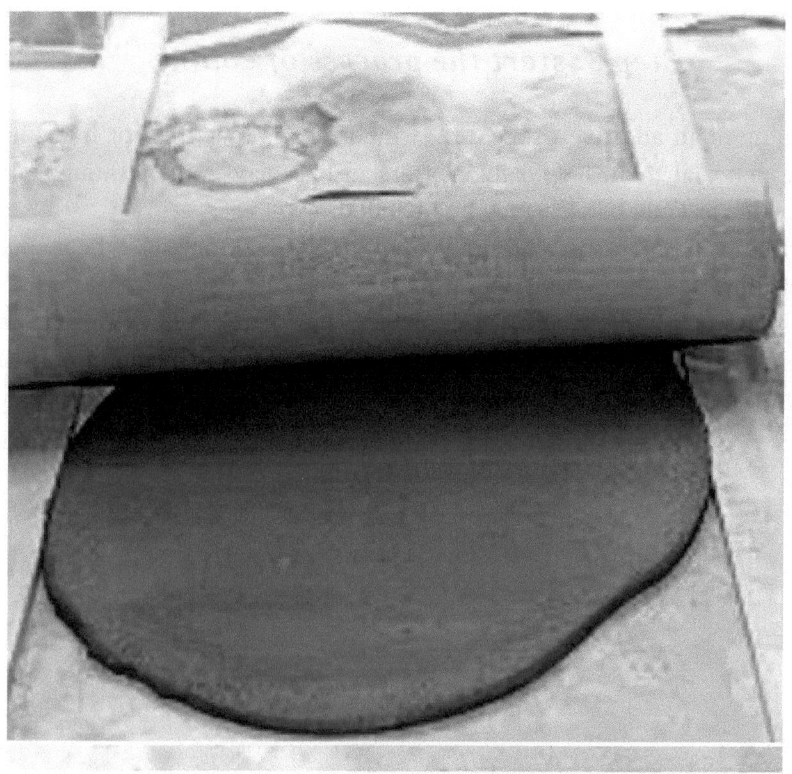

Enter Caption

Pot

A coiled pot's floor or bottom is often a slab or patty of clay that is the same thickness as the final pot. When the bottom slab is rolled out, it should be much bigger than the diameter of the sculpture, since it will be cut afterwards.

Once the slab is complete, set it on a support surface that will enable it to be transported securely. This support surface might be a bat or a bisqued clay disc in the case of a flat-bottomed pot. Utilize a puki, which is a bowl-shaped mold made of plaster, wood, or bisqueware, to create a pot with a curved bottom.

If a puki is not available, a conventional bowl of the appropriate size and slope might be used. Before putting the clay slab in the bowl, line it with several layers of newspaper or linen.

Step 3: start the process of coiling

Coiling is an additive procedure, which means that the pot is made by adding material to it. Typically, potters utilize clay coils, although other forms, such as little patties, may be included.

Working the piece on a turntable, banding wheel, or kick wheel speeds up and simplifies the coiling operation.

Coiling starts on the pot's top surface, not at the sides. This method results in a much stronger joint. Place the first coil on the slab floor, then cut away any extra slab and weld the slab's outside edge into the coil.

Step 4: How to Add Coils to Your Pot

Enter Caption

Row-in-row welding of soft clay is possible. On both the inside and outside of the wall, the strongest joints are welded. The conventional welding method is to use one thumb on the inner surface, going downward, and your fingers on the outside surface, moving upward, to weld the clay. If the clay has solidified in any way, score each joining surface, brush on slurry or slip, and then lay and solder the coil row.

When coils are welded together, the resulting wall thins and stretches outward. The more forceful the welding, the thinner and more expansive the walls. Coils may need to be much thicker at the start than the completed wall. As a general rule, smaller pots utilize coils with a diameter of 3/8 to 1 inch; larger pots use coils with a diameter of 3/4 to 1 1/2 inches.

Step 5: Taking a break

Enter Caption

Coiled shapes may take longer to make than the amount of time provided in a single session. When you must leave your work in progress, line the top row with moist paper towels and then cover the whole piece with plastic.

Allow minor spaces where the plastic hits the table or shelf if you want the bottom of the pot to firm somewhat. In the absence of it, tuck the plastic behind the supporting surface. Add a layer of newspaper or fabric between the pot and the plastic if the humidity is high. This will absorb any moisture that can cause your pot to collapse.

Step 6: Inward Movement

The clay's natural tendency is to expand and migrate outward. Apply a coil to the inner surface of the highest row to draw the wall inward. To complement this direction shift, it is sometimes beneficial to solder the applied coil's top inward and the internal side downward.

As you go to the last row of your pot, you may discover that the welding procedure left your rim overly thin. If this is the case, just add another coil and solder it to either the outside or inner surface of the rim.

Your pot's shape may be perfect at this point, or you may modify it more and thin the walls even more if desired. During the soft leather-hard stage, you may continue working the clay using a paddle and anvil or rib and hand methods.

CHAPTER SIX

Constructing a Simple Slab Pot

Create a Slab

Enter Caption

You'll want to make a thick slurry before starting your slab pot. (Allow several days for clay scraps to fully dry before placing them in a jar with just enough water to cover them. They will dissolve rapidly, forming a slurry.) By substituting slurry for water in the joint, you boost the joint's strength throughout the construction process and throughout the pot's life.

You may press out slabs for tiny pots. Compress a lump of clay into a two-inch-diameter ball. Flatten the ball as much and as evenly as possible using your hands.

Arrange the clay pancake on a work area covered with canvas. Continue smoothing it out with your hand on the work surface or by hammering on it. The finished clay pancake should be uniform in thickness, between 1/4 and 1/2 inch. Lift the slab carefully away from your work surface.

Roll out slabs with a rolling pin to create a bigger pot.

Construct the Slab Pot's Base

Enter Caption

Trim the slab you just formed with your potter's needle. Although you may construct this in almost any size or form you like, for your first slab pot, we propose a foundation that is about two inches by two inches square. (This does not need to be an exact square or precise dimensions. You may eyeball it if you choose.)

Smooth the sliced edges of the square slightly with a quick touch on your work surface. Score (or scrape) the slab's top surface along each edge with your potter's needle. Your scoring should not exceed 1/4 inch in width and 1/16 inch in depth.

Create the Slab Pot's First and Second Sides

Enter Caption

Just like you did in Step One, shape a slab. Using the potter's needle, trim one edge to a straight line. Placing it so that it abuts one side of your foundation, mark and cut away the excess clay to equalize the width of the new slab. Trim the top edge to the desired height for the completed pot.

Create a second slab and trim it to match the first side slab's measurements.

Attach the Slab Pot's First Two Sides

Enter Caption

Score the side slab's bottom edge. Score the inside surface of the final pot along the two side edges. Brush a line of slurry along the scoring on one side of the foundation slab using your sumi brush. Gently insert the upright side slab into the slurried scoring.

At this size, the side slab should be able to sustain itself, but if it does, you can prop it up with any convenient item.

Form a very small coil, about 1/16 inch in diameter. It should be positioned parallel to and inside the inner corner created by the base and side slabs. Lightly press and solder the coil to both the base and side slabs using the rounded end of your wooden tool. Leave any leftover coil length connected but loose.

Rep with the second side slab, being careful to score the internal surface.

Create the Slab Pot's last two sides

Just like you did with Steps One and Three, shape a slab. Using the potter's needle, trim one edge to a straight line. Lay it against one edge of the foundation and mark and cut away the excess clay so that the new slab fits snugly between the internal surfaces of the two already-installed sides. Trim the top edge to the desired height for the completed pot.

Create a second slab and trim it in the same manner as the first.

Attach the Slab Pot's Final Two Sides

Enter Caption

One of the side slabs' bottom and side edges should be scored. Brush a line of slurry along the scoring on each edge using your sumi brush. Gently insert the side slab into the slot formed by the previous two slabs.

Any coil left over after joining the first two slabs should be positioned such that it runs up the side joint. If it is insufficiently long, roll and arrange an additional length such that a coil spans the length of the seam between the side slabs. Using the rounded end of your wooden tool and one hand, gently push and solder the coil to both side slabs. Carry out the same procedure with the joints at the base and on the other side.

Rep with the last side slab, being careful to score the internal surface.

Complete Your Basic Slab Pot

To reinforce the pot's resistance to cracking and breaking, use the rounded end of the wooden tool to gently solder the outside surface of each joint. Gently tap the bottom edges of your pot at an angle to your work surface to help smooth them out and produce a little beveled slope where the pot will lay on a table. (This tiny bevel adds visual lift to the pot, making it more attractive to the eye.)

If the top edge of your pot is uneven, trim the excess using your potter's needle. Bear in mind that you should use your fingers to hold the pot's sides against the needle's pressure. Smooth the top edge by moistening your fingers with slurry and gently running them over it. With your fingers, weld and smooth each top joint together, being careful to hold the clay with one hand while applying pressure with the other.

How to Dry Your Basic Slab Pot

Enter Caption

Clay should not be burnt until it reaches the point of becoming bone dry. To determine whether this is the case, take up your pot and feel it all around. If the surface feels chilly to the touch, it is not completely dry. (The coolness is caused by the evaporation of water from the clay body.)

Drying time is dependent on the relative humidity of the air. Generally, it takes one to two weeks for a pot to dry entirely. If a pot dries quicker than that, loosely cover it with plastic. Too rapid drying might result in the pot shattering. Bear in mind that greenware is quite delicate; dry your pots in an area where they will not be moved, bumped, or jostled.

Once your pot is completely dry, it is ready for bisque firing. Once bisqued, you may add underglazes and glazes and then re-fire your pottery.

CHAPTER SEVEN

How to produce a Pinch Pot Bowl

The fundamental approach for creating a pinch pot bowl is the same as described before. Essentially, you're building a pinch pot, but bigger and with more clay. Additionally, you will be adding a foot ring if desired. And you'll probably spend more time perfecting the bowl's appearance. Unless, of course, you want a rustic bowl that looks really organic. Which does have its own appeal.

Here are some tools that can come in handy:

- Tools for Modeling
- Ribbed Serrated
- Rib Made of Metal
- Ribs of Rubber
- Platter Instrument
- Shredder
- Paddle Made of Wood
- Ceramic Bat
- Wheel for Banding

If you lack these tools and want to begin, have no fear. You should be able to come up with some workable solutions from inside your house. I'll mention a few of these choices as I go through the procedure step by step in the next section.

Step-by-Step Instructions for Making a Pinch Pot Bowl

This is a detailed tutorial on how to make a pinch pot bowl:

Step 1 – Getting Started

Form your clay into an even-shaped ball by rolling and patting it. As said before, you must hold the ball of clay in one hand. Then insert your thumb into the clay's core. Because you're using more clay than you would for a little pinch pot, you'll need to push your thumb firmly into the clay.

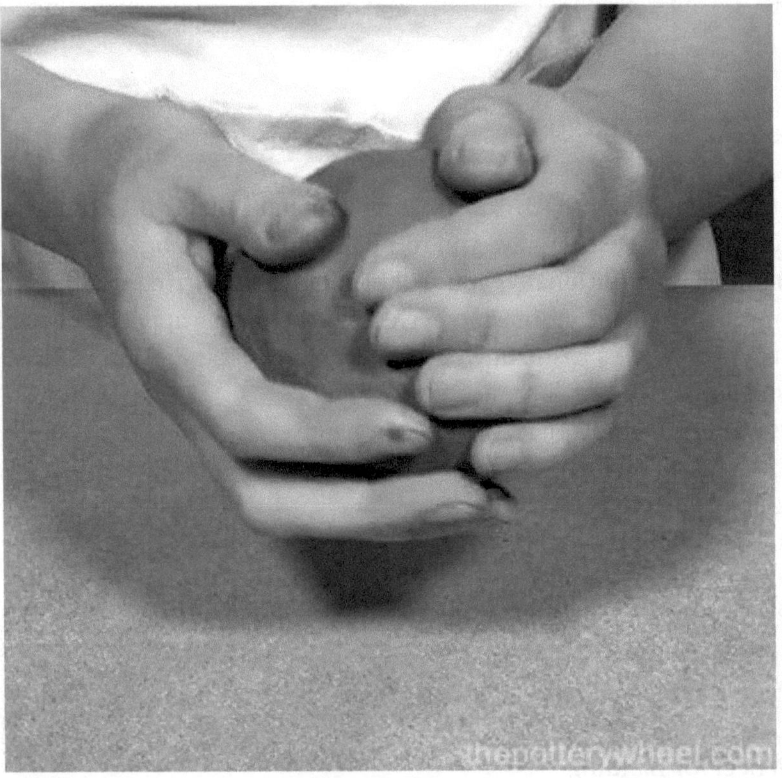

Enter Caption

If you have small hands or are using a huge ball, your thumb will most likely not reach nearly deep enough. That's great; I'll explain how to make the base of your pot sufficiently thin in a minute.

Step 2 – Pinching the Clay

When your thumb is as deep as it will go, begin pinching the clay ball's side. Pinch the length of your fingers together and spin to gradually open the clay ball.

Step 3 – Base and Wall Thinning

Once the clay has opened up somewhat, you will be able to feel whether the pot's base is rather thick. If the thickness of the clay on the foundation exceeds 12 inch, it must be thinned. To do this, you must transfer part of the clay from the base up the pot's walls. Using the tips of your fingers is a simple technique to do this.

Begin by holding the pot with one hand. Then, lightly massage the clay on the pot's base with the tips of your fingers. The stroking action should begin at the base of the pot and work its way up the pot's walls. While doing so, part of the clay in the base will be drawn up the pot's side. This will result in a thinning of the base's wall.

Once a few strokes in one direction are completed, flip the pot and continue. By twisting the pot, an equal quantity of clay from the base is distributed evenly throughout the bowl's diameter. If you continue stroking in the same spot, the clay will eventually accumulate on one side of the bowl.

In your supporting hand, you will begin to feel the bowl's base thinning away. The base will feel lighter, and the tips of your fingers will begin to feel their way through the clay. Caution: Do not overuse it. You want to avoid making the foundation overly thin. Aim to make the bowl's walls uniform in thickness throughout.

Step 4 – Creating the Shape of the Bowl

Turn your bowl over as you work to inspect the overall form. Is it assuming the form that you desire? In this case, I want a bowl with an equal form. As a result, I flipped the bowl over and shaped it with my hands into a half-sphere.

Step 5: Using a Banding Wheel

Using a mix of pinching, stroking, and shaping, repeat this technique. As you do so, the bowl form will expand. Additionally, the edges of your pinch pot bowl will thin and become more equal.

When you're satisfied with the thickness and form of your bowl, invert it on your work area. At this time, it is ideal to support your work using a banding wheel and a pottery bat. A banding wheel is essentially a circular plinth that is spun by hand.

You have mostly been supporting the pinch bowl in your hand up to this point. A banding wheel, on the other hand, will enable you to simply spin your bowl on the work area. By mounting your bowl on a ceramic bat, you may simply carry it after you're completed.

Step 6: Making the Foot Ring

Pat the bowl's base gently with a wood paddle or a standard kitchen spatula. This will flatten the bowl's base, allowing it to sit level on your table.

Then, around the thickness of your pinky finger, roll a coil of clay. This coil will form the bowl's foot ring, therefore it must be trimmed to the proper length. Drape the coil over the base of the bowl, indicating the location of the foot ring. Then trim the coil's ends to the desired length.

Enter Caption

After cutting your clay coil to the desired length, scrape the coil's ends using a serrated rib tool. If you are unable to get a serrated instrument, a kitchen fork will suffice. The purpose of scratching the clay's surface is to aid in the secure bonding of the two ends. Thus, anything that scuffs and scratches the clay's surface will work.

Once the surface has been scored, paint some clay slip on either end of the coil. Clay slip is just a mixture of clay and water to create liquid clay. Here are several simple methods for creating clay slip.

After scoring and slipping the coil's ends, connect the two surfaces. With your fingers, blend the clay together to create a smooth donut form from the coil. Arrange the clay coil on the bowl's base, but do not yet bind it to the bowl. Rather than that, gently pinch the coil into the form you choose for the foot ring. Wrap the bowl and foot ring in a loose plastic bag and let it to firm up overnight.

Step 7 – Organize the Interior Surface

The next day, determine how solid the clay has grown. If it remains soft, remove it from the bag and set it out in the open. Take care that it does not get too hard and dry on a hot or dry day.

Once the clay is almost leather hard, you may begin cleaning the bowl's surfaces. Begin by scraping the interior of the bowl's surface to remove any clay lumps and bumps. Use the back of a metal kitchen spoon as a guide. Alternatively, use any tool that matches the contour of your bowl's inside.

If you're looking to purchase a tool for this task, the Mudtools platter rib is a decent option. That is what I am utilizing in this image. It's ideal for this operation since the tool's curvature fits exactly within the bowl. This results in a silky finish.

As you can see, I'm also placing the bowl on a piece of foam on the table. This prevents the bowl's base from flattening out on the hard surface.

I also use a mix of a metal rib tool and a soft rubber rib to smooth the surface. To begin, I use the metal rib to scrape the surface. Then I use a rubber rib to smooth the surface. This combination of equipment will result in a very smooth, satin-finish compressed clay.

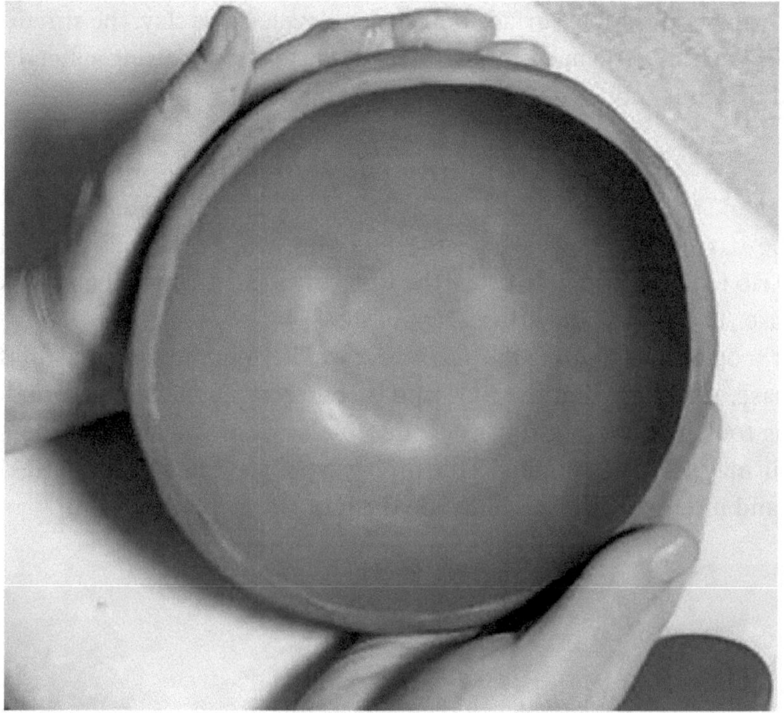

Enter Caption

By the way, if you like this, you may be interested in learning how to construct a pinch pot teapot.

If you're interested, you can grab my ebook for free here. It's a comprehensive step-by-step instruction to creating a pinch pot teapot...

Step 8 – Organize the Exterior Surface

The next stage in creating a pinch pot is to clean up the bowl's outside. A simple approach to do this is to use a shredder to eliminate any lumps or bumps on the outside. A shredder is essentially a rasp that aids in the removal of superfluous clay from leather hard clay. Alternatively, you may use a shredder designed specifically for pottery. The Mudtools shredder is one example of this. However, a comparable instrument is available at most local hardware stores. The one I'm using in this photo is just a shredder I bought up at a home improvement shop.

Gently run the shredder over the outside of the pinch pot bowl to eliminate any undesirable surface defects. On leveled-out clay, the shredder will leave a texture. You may simply remove this texture by using a metal rib followed by a soft rubber rib.

Step 9: Attaching the Foot Ring

Score the base of the bowl where the foot ring will be affixed using the serrated rib tool. Additionally, score the foot ring's side that will be attached to the base. Then, on both surfaces, apply slip.

After scoring and slipping the surfaces, carefully put the foot ring on the bowl's base. Ascertain that the foot ring is centered. Then, using a wooden modeling tool, mix the foot ring's clay into the bowl. If you lack a modeling tool, you may use the rounded end of a teaspoon's handle. On both the outside and interior of the join, include the foot ring.

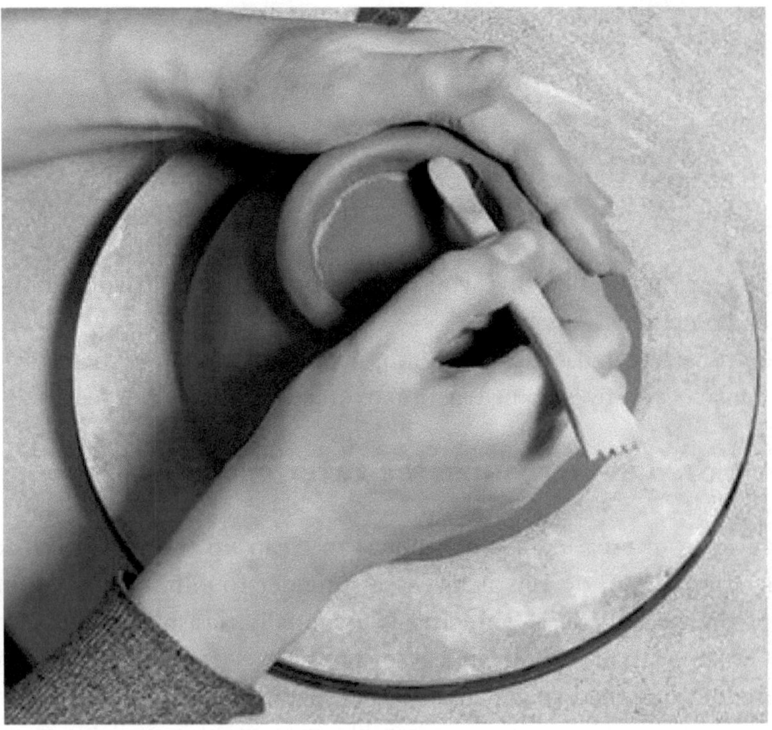

Enter Caption

Once the foot ring is joined, you may use your rib tools to smooth up the connection once again.

Additionally, the foot ring should be cut and leveled to ensure that the bowl rests securely on the table. The simplest method to do this is to shred any surplus clay using the shredding tool. Simply run the shredder down the bottom of the foot ring until it reaches the desired depth. Additionally, to ensure that the bowl sits evenly on the work area. Again, the shredder markings may be readily erased with your regular tools.

Step 10 – Rim Leveling and Final Touches

When creating a pinch pot, one of the last tasks is to level off the bowl's rim. This is accomplished by the use of a mix of shredder and rib tools. I use the shredder to remove excess material off the rim. I do, however, run it around the inside and outer edges of the rim to flatten down the lip. A large rim might seem incomplete. Thus, cutting a little amount of the clay off each side of the lip might give it a more polished appearance.

Another tool I use to polish the rim is a homemade gizmo. I cut some curved parts from a vintage library card. I've discovered that the simplest method to do this is to cut off the curves using a pair of scissors. Then, using a tiny piece of sanding paper, smooth the snipped-out plastic parts.

The card's snipped-out curve may then be run around the bowl's rim. This eliminates any uneven lumps and bumps in the clay, leaving a smooth, curving lip.

Enter Caption

Finally, wrap a little moist piece of chamois leather around the bowl's lip. This removes any little markings left by your instruments or your fingertips. Additionally, you may run this around the foot ring to clean it up. It is essential that the chamois leather be somewhat moist. If you use a very wet chamois, it will deposit an excessive amount of slip on the surface of your clay.

And here is the completed work. Mayco Elements, Copper Adventurine was used to glaze it. Additionally, a little amount of gold leaf has been put to the lip.

Enter Caption

Printed by Libri Plureos GmbH in Hamburg,
Germany